KNIFE THROWING

KNIFE THROWING
A Practical Guide

by HARRY K. McEVOY

CHARLES E. TUTTLE COMPANY
Rutland · Vermont : Tokyo · Japan

Representatives

For Continental Europe:
BOXERBOOKS, INC., *Zurich*

For the British Isles:
PRENTICE-HALL INTERNATIONAL, INC., *London*

For Australasia:
PAUL FLESCH & CO., PTY. LTD., *Melbourne*

For Canada:
HURTIG PUBLISHERS, *Edmonton*

Published by the Charles E. Tuttle Company, Inc.
of Rutland, Vermont & Tokyo, Japan
with editorial offices at
Suido 1-chome, 2-6, Bunkyo-ku, Tokyo

Copyright in Japan, 1973
by Charles E. Tuttle Co., Inc.

Library of Congress Catalog Card No. 72-91550
International Standard Book No. 0-8048 1099-0

First printing, 1973
Third printing, 1974

Printed in Japan

Dedicated to good sportsmen everywhere
—past and present—
who have taken the time to learn and
enjoy the fascinating art of knife throwing.
May their blades never rust!

TABLE OF CONTENTS

7

LIST OF ILLUSTRATIONS

9

KNIFE THROWING

1. Author demonstrating the professional throw.

IT'S FUN TO THROW A KNIFE

It's fun to throw a knife. Not only is knife throwing fun, it is also great sport, entertainment, recreation, a body developer, a mind relaxer, and a stimulant— all rolled into one! It can also be a wonderful hobby, pastime, or even a profession, depending on how you go about it.

Practically any man, woman, or child from an early age on up can learn to throw a knife with skill and accuracy. All it takes is practice once the fundamentals are mastered.

These fundamentals are easy to learn because anyone who can throw a stick, baseball, or rock, crack a whip, or cast a spinning rod can also quickly learn to throw a knife. The only other requirement for successful knife throwing is to use a weapon that is properly designed and balanced and is of sufficient length and weight for maximum control.

Sportsmen knife throwers are increasing in numbers every year at a rapid pace. From the early 1950s, when suitable throwing knives were designed and became available for the first time, to the present day, when various throwing types have been perfected and widely distributed by top-notch cutlery dealers throughout the United States, knife throwing as a modern sport has grown and thrived.

Perhaps this rapid growth of interest in knife throwing is because the sport is fundamentally still a back yard recreational activity, with only a small amount of throwing room needed. The fairly recent availability of inexpensive, well balanced, and virtually unbreakable throwing-knives has also helped.

Less obvious reasons—but important ones—are the desire of growing numbers of sportsmen to use the throwing-knife as a hunting weapon, which necessitates considerable back-yard practice, and the interest generated by many returning servicemen, who took up the sport with deadly seriousness while overseas.

Vast numbers of throwing-knives were airmailed to servicemen stationed in Viet Nam from dealers in the United States, and these special weapons served a double purpose. They relieved the boredom of camp life by providing recreation and also helped many a G.I. in a desperate, close-quarter combat situation.

As a modern sport, knife throwing has many

advantages. All a sportsman needs is a good knife—or set of knives—designed for the purpose, whether made to throw by the handle or balanced to throw by the blade. Both techniques will be fully described in the following pages. A suitable target is cheap and easy to construct, and only a small portion of the back yard is needed for the throwing range.

There is hardly any other sport that can provide so much recreational pleasure at such small cost as knife throwing. It can be enjoyed as a "solo" activity or can be expanded to include other throwers for keen competition.

A certain amount of care and several appropriate safety measures are required in practicing the sport, since spectators are drawn "like bees to honey" whenever a serious knife thrower goes out back for a practice session. This should not, however, present any great problem, and suggestions will be offered herein that will enable the thrower to deal with the situation.

The art and science of professional knife throwing will also be fully described and explained, although it is for the sportsmen knife throwers, who may someday outnumber the professionals by more than a million to one, that this book is primarily written.

It's fun to throw a knife because it is a sport in which individual skills can be developed to a very high degree. And remember that anyone who can throw a stick, stone, or baseball can also learn to throw a knife. There is no great "mystery" that has to be revealed. Expert knife throwing, like great proficiency in any other sport, is developed by natural aptitude and instinct combined with that one magic ingredient:

LOTS OF PRACTICE!

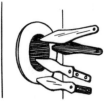

CHOICE OF WEAPONS

As every sportsman knows, regardless of his favorite sport, a high degree of achievement is more easily attained if the sportsman is using the best equipment he can get. Top performers in the fields of archery, skeet, trap, golf, and tennis, to mention only a few, use the finest tools of their sport they can afford. In most cases this pays off in extra dividends of personal satisfaction and increased skill.

The same is true of knife throwing.

Not every knife is suitable for throwing. The elements of length, weight, and balance in a proper combination of all three determine just how good the weapon is for throwing, regardless of whether it is designed to be hurled by handle or by blade.

First and foremost is to have a knife that is properly balanced for throwing. Next in importance is weight, in proportion to balance and length, for the knife must have enough "heft" to enable it to penetrate and stick in the target. And finally, it must be long enough to give the knife thrower maximum control over his throw.

The "rule of thumb" method in selecting a good throwing knife is to pick one *which weighs approximately one ounce for every inch of overall length*. The recommended limits for the most efficient throwing-knives are from 10 to 15 inches, with corresponding weights from 10 to 16 ounces. Knives over the one-pound limit require a thrower with a very strong pitching arm.

The most important factor, however, is that of balance. For instance, a knife may be perfectly balanced for the job for which it was designed, such as the delicate task of skinning or dressing out game, but it may be balanced incorrectly for chopping lettuce or slicing bread.

A good throwing-knife *has* to be balanced for throwing. If it is designed to be thrown by the handle, point first, the pointed end is the heavy end, with the balancing point at the approximate overall center, or up to one inch back of the center. With this type of knife the thrower will hurl the weapon for one, two, or even several spins to strike his target point first (Fig. 2).

If the knife is designed to be thrown by the blade, it will usually resemble a slim-bladed hunting knife with a light point and heavy handle. In this style weapon the balancing point should be within an inch

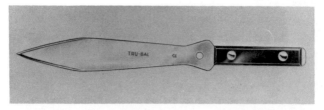

2. Knife designed and balanced to be thrown by the handle.

3. Knife designed to be thrown by the blade.

either way of the hilt or crosspiece dividing the blade from the handle. With this type of throwing-knife, the thrower will have $\frac{1}{2}$ spin, $1\frac{1}{2}$ spins, $2\frac{1}{2}$ spins, etc., to hurl his blade into the target point first (Fig. 3).

Of the two types, it is easier for the beginning knife thrower to start with the handle-throwing style since only even spins are involved. But when he also masters the type hurled by the blade, handle first, he will greatly enjoy throwing it, even though it is more difficult to stick squarely. This difficulty is caused by the weight of the rapidly spinning handle which on an imperfect throw or slightly misjudged distance may flip the knife up and out of the bull's-eye.

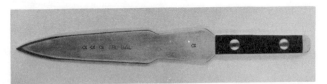

4. "Game-getter" knife, for use in hunting small game.

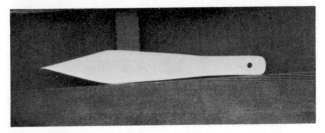

5. The Paul LaCross professional throwing-knife.

For best results the heavy end of a throwing-knife should always be thrown first, with the lighter end gripped by the hand. In this way the thrower can hurl his weapon with maximum force and velocity and at the same time have better control for accuracy.

There are a few rare throwing-knives that can be hurled equally well by handle or blade. Knives of this type are especially designed as "game getters" or "combat throwers," and are used for hunting game with a throwing-knife or for military combat emergencies (Fig. 4). Some professional types, such as the one designed and used by Paul LaCross, the great professional knife thrower, are also perfectly balanced to be thrown equally well by handle or blade (Fig. 5). These knives are balanced at approximately dead center of the overall length and are superbly designed to achieve the right combination of length, weight, and balance.

The most important point to remember, however, is to select a knife designed and balanced for throwing, between 10 and 15 inches overall, with a recommended length at around $13\frac{1}{2}$ inches. The weight of the knife should average approximately one ounce for every inch of overall length, regardless of which type you choose. A throwing-blade that meets the above specifications is usually a good one for the sport. After he gets his knife, the rest is up to the thrower.

HOW TO THROW A KNIFE

It has been pointed out that knife throwing is fun. It is also easy to learn the techniques of throwing a knife providing the thrower has the ability to hurl a rock, stick, or baseball.

Handle grip

Before any sportsman can learn to throw a knife properly, however, he first must know how to grip the weapon. He will start out using either the handle grip or the blade grip, depending upon which style of throwing-knife he has chosen.

Since the handle-throwing type is the easiest to throw, it is this model that will be considered first.

After you have selected a knife of the proper length, weight, and balance—one that "feels" right to you—you should grasp the handle firmly in the same natural manner in which you would normally grasp

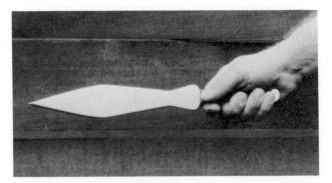

6. The handle grip, for sportsman's style of throwing.

a hatchet handle. The ball of your thumb is pressed against the rivet nearest the hilt, and your fingers are curled firmly and comfortably around the handle (Fig. 6). With a target in position and you standing at a distance of approximately 15 feet from the bull's eye, you should now be ready to try that first practice throw.

Keeping the plane of the knife *vertical* as it leaves your hand, pitch the weapon hard and fast with an overhand throw, letting it slip out of your hand when you instinctively feel that it is lined up properly with the target.

The results of that first throw are not too important because, before you can expect to attain proficiency as a knife thrower, it is necessary to understand thoroughly the mechanics of the throw and the simple techniques involved.

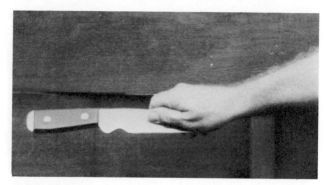

7. The blade grip, for sportsman's style of throwing, showing position of thumb.

Blade grip

When throwing by the blade, assuming you have selected a weapon designed and balanced for this style of throwing, you grasp the blade of the knife firmly—cutting edge away from the palm of your hand—with the thumb pointed directly towards the handle. Your first, second, and third fingers are lined up on the opposite side of the blade, while the little finger can be curled up and out of the way. It is too short to be of much help anyway (Figs. 7–9).

From the bottom finger to the tip of the point, an inch or so of steel should protrude. This will bring the point to within $\frac{1}{2}$ inch of the crease in your skin where hand and wrist are joined. It will also permit much better control of the knife than if you grasped it at the extreme tip of the point.

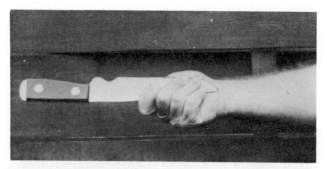

8. The blade grip, showing alignment of fingers.

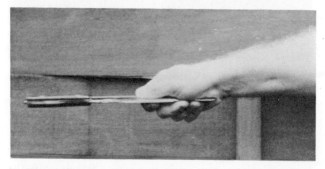

9. The blade grip, showing the full grip for throwing in the sportsman's style.

The throw is then made with the plane of the knife *horizontal*. This is the method recommended for the thrower who is using a weapon with one sharp edge. With a professional style of throwing-knife, of the design favored by true professionals of the art, there are no sharp edges involved. The blade throw is

10. (*left*). Author demonstrating the professional stance for the handle throw.

11. (*right*). Professional stance for the blade throw.

practically the same as the handle throw, in which case, of course, the knife is *always* thrown with the plane of the blade *vertical* (Figs. 10, 11). But professional throwing techniques differ somewhat from those used by sportsmen and will be considered in depth in Chapter VIII.

The game of baseball offers the best example of illustrating the basic points of knife throwing, because in the overhand pitch the mechanics of the movements are about the same. Four elements are involved: stance; wind-up; throw; and follow-through.

12. The stance.

Using the handle throw, the handle is grasped by the method described previously—firm grip, ball of thumb on rivet nearest the hilt, and fingers curled naturally around the handle. The plane of the blade should be *vertical* when it leaves your hand.

Stance

Your stance is like that of a righthanded baseball pitcher—right foot forward on the "mound," at a distance of four or five paces or approximately 15 feet from the target (Fig. 12).

13. The wind-up.   14. The throw.

Wind-up and throw

With a natural wind-up for a hard, fast throw with full power and velocity, you swing your body and left leg forward in the throwing movement while your knife arm swings back, up, and forward in a smooth circular sweep toward the target. The throw is very similar to an overhand pitch or cracking a bull whip, but without the usual wrist snap. The knife should slip from your hand just before you reach the end of your swing, at the split second you instinctively know it is lined up with the bull's-eye (Figs. 13, 14).

15. The follow-through.

Follow-through

The follow-through is a continuation of the throwing movement *after* the knife has slipped from your hand. It is carried out to the end of your full, natural swing. Knife-throwing experts, both professionals and sportsmen alike, agree completely that the follow-through is the real secret of guiding your knife accurately to the target (Fig. 15).

Remember that the knife must leave your hand with no wrist snap. A good rule is to let it slip from your grasp as though it were red-hot! This thought at the moment of release should do much to eliminate any potential wrist snap in the throw.

Your distance from the target

Since no knife flies as an arrow flies, but spins naturally end-over-end similar to a pinwheel (except in an underhand "bowling" throw of three or four feet from the target), it is necessary first to find the exact distance you must stand away from the target for a successful throw and then to mark the spot so that you can stand on it each time. This is one factor that must remain constant for each distance thrown, whether you are hurling the blade for a half spin or are using the quintuple spin sometimes necessary when hunting game or giving demonstrations of your knife-throwing prowess.

If you are left-handed, the technique is the same but adapted to the left-handed stance.

Now your throw has been made. If the knife struck the target squarely, point first, you have already found your correct distance to stand each time for a successful throw. If the blade hit flat against the target with the point upward, it is necessary to step *backward* a foot or two. If it hit flat with the point downward, you must step *forward* a foot or two. If the knife struck the target handle first, you must experiment a foot or two backward or forward on each throw until the weapon strikes the target squarely, point first. Now you have found your "spot." Dig a hole, drive a stake, but make sure that spot is marked. Pace off the distance and memorize it to the inch because from now on, you are a knife thrower!

Proper coordination, which includes perfect timing and rhythm in your swing, release, and follow-through, is necessary for each successful throw. Accuracy is developed only by practice.

Target distance for blade grip

The technique in throwing by the blade grip varies somewhat from handle throwing techniques because there is an extra half spin involved after the weapon leaves your hand. First, you must find your "distance" during a preliminary throw. If you have been standing four or five paces from the target for the handle throw on a single revolution of the knife, try six or seven paces for the blade throw of $1\frac{1}{2}$ spins. You need the extra pace or two since the weapon will be leaving your hand handle first, and it should be thrown with the plane of the blade *horizontal*.

If you have accurately determined your distance for the $1\frac{1}{2}$ spin throw and hit the target squarely, point first, you have quickly learned the basic technique for throwing a sharp-edged knife by the blade. If it failed to stick, you must again experiment backward or forward, as in the handle throw, until you have found your exact spot upon which to stand each time for a successful blade throw. Again, memorize and mark that distance to the inch and make it a point to throw from that same distance every time you hurl the knife by the blade for a $1\frac{1}{2}$ spin throw.

Extending the target distance

Eventually the time will come when you will want to stick the knife at a greater distance, such as a double spin by the handle or $2\frac{1}{2}$ spins by the blade. Regardless of the number of spins involved, the knife should always be thrown hard and fast with your full velocity and power; and, of course, with a greater distance to the target involved, the more power the better!

The additional distance required to get that extra spin averages out to about three paces. For example, if you get a perfect single-spin throw by the handle at five paces, you can expect to get a perfect double spin at eight paces. The same rule applies to the blade throw when increasing the range from $1\frac{1}{2}$ to $2\frac{1}{2}$ spins. And the same for a triple spin, and so on.

The reason you need five full paces for the single spin handle throw as opposed to eight paces for the double spin throw is that the movement of the body and knife hand forward from the original stance consumes about two paces of the distance before the weapon actually leaves your hand. The knife in flight may make its complete turn in three paces from the target, or a double turn in six paces from the target; but you have to add the additional two paces for the mechanics of the throw, regardless of one, two, three, or more spins, up to the maximum controllable distance of five spins. You will have to allow for the greater distances involved in multiple spins by increasing the trajectory or line of flight of the knife, the same as you would were you throwing a baseball 100 feet instead of only half that distance. So remember to throw it hard and fast at *any* distance involving one full spin or more.

You will find, after much practice, that you can keep reasonable control of the thrown knife up to approximately 50 feet. The big job then is to be able to hit the target at that distance, to say nothing of getting the weapon to stick squarely.

Throwing a knife at the longer distances is not too practical for ordinary target practice unless you are training for accuracy in hunting game. The techniques and other points concerning this phase of knife throwing will be explained fully in a later chapter.

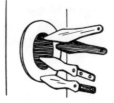

IV

HOW TO DEVELOP
"PIN-POINT" ACCURACY

"What can I do to develop accuracy?" This question becomes uppermost in the mind of a knife thrower when he realizes that sticking a knife consistently somewhere in the target area is far easier than hitting the exact mark at which he aims.

A properly designed, well-balanced throwing-knife will stick practically every time when hurled for one or more spins of the weapon by an experienced knife thrower who knows his own correct distance from the target. Getting that pin-point accuracy, however, is another matter!

Perhaps "pin-point" is the wrong term to use since most target faces are considerably larger than pin-points and usually range in size from a few inches in diameter to a foot or more in width. But even a circular target eight inches across is hard to stick consistently unless you develop and master a "point-of-aim" technique for your knife throwing, similar to that employed by the archers of old with their longbows. The point-of-aim in target archery is a "sighting mark" used for indirect aiming of the arrow point to enable the marksman to drop his arrow into the "gold," or bull's-eye, at the regulation distance being shot.

In knife throwing, the point-of-aim is only one of several guiding factors needed to develop complete accuracy. Above all, concentration is essential, but this alone is not enough unless it is combined with other ingredients. One of these is constant practice with one special knife or a matched set. It is exactly the same for top performers in other sports, including archery, golf, bowling, and tennis.

In each of these endeavors, the performer has his favorite "instrument," be it a putting iron, a specially weighted and fitted bowling ball, a tennis racket, or an archery bow. The same is true of a throwing-knife. When you find a knife of a certain design, length, weight, and balance that you feel is "right" for you, you have won half the battle. The rest is practice, concentration, instinct, and—last but not least—that little point-of-aim.

Point-of-aim

Assume you have a throwing-knife that fills you with complete confidence. It feels just right in your hand and throws beautifully. However, although you stick it squarely every time, you can't seem to nail that elusive bull's-eye more than once or twice out of every five or even ten throws. How do you go about correcting the situation?

First of all, walk up to the target and place what almost amounts to the proverbial "pin-point" exactly in the center of your circular target face. This pin-point can be a tiny half-inch circle of white adhesive tape if used against a dark background. If your target face is white, cut your pin-point out of black electrical tape. It is important to position it as closely to the center as possible, because every throw you make from that moment on should be aimed *not* at the target face in general, but at that precise, little pin-point.

All through the various knife-throwing movements —stance, wind-up, throw, and follow-through— keep both eyes fixed steadily upon that tiny, half-inch "point-of-aim" in the center of your target face. Use all your powers of concentration to imagine that the pin-point is a super magnet that will draw your blade irresistibly to it for a perfect, point-first hit.

Now make that first throw. If your knife does not stick in the center or somewhere near the center of the target area, throw over again. Keep throwing, but watch carefully where each throw sticks. Soon you will observe that a "pattern" begins to take shape. Perhaps most of your throws will wind up about three inches to the right of your pin-point, somewhere near the three o'clock position, for example.

It is now a simple matter to start correcting your trouble. Take the adhesive-backed pin-point and move it three inches to the left, placing it at the nine o'clock position on the target face.

Again, concentrate completely on that pin-point, which is your point-of-aim, and try to hit it squarely with each throw. Forget all about the true center of your target face. Think only of your point-of-aim, that little half inch pin-point.

Much sooner than you realize, you will find that your knife is hitting almost dead center into the target face and that your problem is solved.

Once you master this knife-throwing point-of-aim technique, that half-inch pin-point can become strictly imaginary. And with continued practice, concentration, and your natural aptitude and instinct all working together for you, it shouldn't be long before you will be hitting almost everything at which you throw your knife—squarely and on the button.

V

TARGETS: HOW AND WHERE

A good, practical target backstop is a simple thing to build. Your local dealer in used lumber provides an excellent source for target timber at a reasonable price. Sometimes a local sawmill that specializes in rough-sawed lumber is the best source of all because this type of lumber can also be custom-sawed to the desired thickness and width for no extra charge.

Target construction

If at all obtainable, your target boards should be at least three inches thick and as wide as possible—the wider the better, since the target should be a minimum of two feet wide. A three-foot width is much better. If three wide boards are used, the center board can be replaced quickly, as needed, since the center plank will take most of the wear and tear on the target (especially after you achieve that pin-point accuracy!). Also, a board that is at least three inches thick can be turned over and used again without being completely "chewed up" as a thinner plank would be.

The grain of the wood in a knife or tomahawk target should always be vertical. Nail two or three strong crosspieces horizontally across the back of the target boards to hold them tightly together. When you become skilled with a knife, most of your throws will stick in vertical alignment with the grain of the wood, and the same is true for a hatchet or tomahawk throw.

The hanging target

For ordinary use, the knife thrower can build a stand-up type target five or six feet tall which can be leaned or nailed against a tree or other convenient object; or else a more permanent hanging type can be constructed. The recommended length for the hanging target is to measure your boards the distance between eye-level and knee-level.

The hanging target suspended from and against a permanent frame is especially recommended to the serious knife thrower (Figs. 16, 17). It is constructed of three lengths of threaded two-inch pipe joined together by standard pipe "elbows" in the shape of an inverted U. The top bar need be only 18 to 24 inches long, with a heavy eye-bolt secured through the center of the pipe from which the target will be suspended in front of the frame. The target

16. Knife-throwing target of the hanging type.

itself will be considerably wider than the inverted
U-frame and can be as long as the knife thrower
feels is necessary. The upright pipes of the frame
can be seven or eight feet in length and should be
imbedded in concrete to a depth of 18 to 24 inches
below the surface of the ground. This will make a
most excellent and permanent frame for the target.

Heavy staples should be used to attach a short
length of sturdy steel chain across the target's back,
and a strong S-hook should connect the target
chain to the eye-bolt that is fastened through the

17. Rear view of hanging target.

top of the frame. The S-hook and steel chain must be strong enough not only to hold the weight of the target, but also to withstand the considerable strain exerted when the deeply imbedded knives are forcibly withdrawn from the wood.

With this system of suspension, the target can be lifted down from the frame for winter storage when cold weather and snow may make outdoor knife throwing a bit inconvenient. It is also easy to take down the target for repairs or modifications, or for turning it to face the opposite direction.

Target materials

Several types of wood can be used to build targets. Soft white or sugar pine is the best whenever it can be obtained. Soft maple, poplar, basswood, willow, and redwood can also be used. In the southern U.S.A. a good target can be made of cypress. Even elm is used if the other varieties are not available, but the so-called "soft" woods are by far the most desirable, especially basswood.

Positioning target faces

Since most knife throwers use a set of three or more matched knives, it is recommended that three target faces—or one for each knife thrown—be placed in vertical alignment (Fig. 16). The target board should be of sufficient length to accommodate at least three target faces without crowding. Depending on the final size and shape of the target, it is wise to plan a separate target face for each knife used in the set. If you throw more than one knife at the same bull's-eye, you will quickly nick your weapons or clobber the handles. This should be avoided, always. It is also recommended that target faces be placed no higher than eye-level.

Other target objects

Many objects will serve as suitable targets, including large stumps of wood, dead tree trunks, and the butt end of a large, sawed log, which also makes an especially good target for tomahawk or hatchet throwing. The best targets are flat and not rounded. Be sure to avoid using utility or telephone poles, or even live trees, for objects upon which to demonstrate your skill. The owners of such items take a dim view of damage done to their property even if no harm was intended.

Moving targets

Once you have acquired the necessary proficiency with the thrown knife on stationary targets, you can start on moving targets. These provide tremendous sport and a keen challenge. They also help to condition you for the sport of hunting game with the thrown knife, which is one of the few sports that can provide a thrill somewhat comparable to fighting a bull, wrestling an alligator, or catching a giant blue marlin.

Moving targets are easy to build and very inexpensive. One type can be made from an old tire casing. With scrap lumber at least two inches thick, you cut the pieces so that they will fit snugly inside the casing. Hold the target firmly together by crosspieces nailed across the back. A painted bull's-eye provides the mark. This target can be rolled in front of the thrower or suspended by a rope or chain from the branch of a convenient tree. It can then be spun or swung back and forth. When you find you can hit the bull's-eye five out of ten throws while the apparatus is in motion, you can consider yourself an accomplished knife thrower, ready for hunting or public exhibitions.

Sliding targets

The sliding target is greatly favored, especially by riflemen and archers, but it is also valuable as a training device for knife throwers practicing for the hunt. This is usually a square or rectangular target with two strong screw eyes fastened into the top edge of a thick board. These screw eyes are threaded on a tight wire suspended at eye level above the ground. The target slides along the wire slowly or rapidly, depending on how hard it is pushed from its starting position. Not only does this type of moving target provide great sport, but it is also a most excellent device for training a knife thrower in split-second timing and precision. He must have both if he ever expects to bag even small game, which usually moves quickly.

Whether you decide to hunt with a throwing-knife or not, moving targets have the virtue of novelty and provide an exceptional challenge to a knife thrower's skill.

Multiple target field rounds

The 28-target field round, or hunting round, used by field archers suggests a fine novelty event for knife throwers. Up to now field archers have always especially enjoyed the Big Game Round, in which life-sized targets of various game animals are used.

This round provides so much fun for bowmen that knife throwers might wish to adopt the basic idea for their own sport.

Archers have four shots at the larger animal target faces, many with "walk-up" positions. In real hunting the archer has a very great advantage over the knife thrower since, as already noted, no knife ever flies as an arrow does but must, of course, turn end-over-end on its flight to the mark. An arrow can be shot many times the effective range of a throwing-knife, and if an archer misses his quarry, he often has a chance for another shot or two before the game moves in fright.

The 28-target field or hunting round of archers, however, requires a considerable amount of acreage, while the knife thrower can lay out a course of as many targets as he needs in his own back yard. These can be small targets with animal faces tacked to the boards and nailed to stakes driven into the ground. Any archery shop can provide the target faces at a nominal cost. With a little imagination, the knife thrower can rig up numerous interesting animal targets for use at various distances and devise rules to govern contestants for a good competitive event.

Indoor targets

If the regular knife target is moved indoors for the winter, and space is available in a basement or heated garage, cover the walls and floor with old carpets to protect the weapons from being marred on the hard cement. Everybody misses a "stick" once in a while.

Keep your targets in good repair and don't worry about getting them rain-soaked. A waterlogged target will soften somewhat, a phenomenon that is especially favorable to the knife thrower if the target is constructed of rather hard wood. Wipe the points dry after each throw to prevent rust.

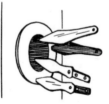

VI

TOMAHAWKS AND BOWIES

It is much easier to learn how to throw a tomahawk or hatchet than it is to throw a knife. In fact, from a practical standpoint, the easiest way to master the mechanics of knife throwing is to learn first how to hurl a hatchet or tomahawk. This is because the "hatchet throw" is basically identical to the overhand handle throw with a knife. If you have already mastered the art of knife throwing, it is very simple to master the hatchet throw almost immediately.

The tomahawk is uniquely constructed to bring out the best possible combination of weight and balance for throwing purposes (Fig. 18). Compact in design, light in weight, and deadly in the hands of a skilled American Indian warrior, the weapon was a wicked tool for throwing and hand-to-hand combat. For centuries it was used in the primeval forests and plains of the North American continent

18. Tomahawks.

by Indians and white frontiersmen alike, as a last-resort protection.

Unlike the hatchets and battle axes of early Europeans, the tomahawk was a primitive American development. Trappers, settlers, and frontiersmen adopted its use rapidly after some grim lessons in Indian warfare. Only when long-range weapons became more reliable did the tomahawk fade from widespread use.

Today there is a revival of interest among sportsmen in this noble weapon as a throwing instrument. Practically everybody who has been a Boy Scout has enjoyed the experience of throwing his Scout hatchet while in camp or on the trail. It was as natural as building a campfire. So, among the vast number of former Boy Scouts who remember the simple technique of throwing a hatchet or tomahawk, there exists a great potential group of tomahawk throwers who can now enjoy the sport as adults.

Stance and grip for tomahawk

The thrower can start with the same basic stance he would use for hurling a knife, since the various elements of the throw are essentially the same. The handle, for the overhand throw, is gripped firmly as though you were chopping kindling. The wind-up consists simply of bringing the hatchet back and then swinging it forward in a natural, overhand throw. As in knife throwing, the handle should slip from your grasp when the weapon is lined up with the target. There is no wrist snap, and the follow-through should be the same as it is with a throwing-knife.

Tomahawk throw

Most tomahawk or hatchet throwers are content to hurl their weapon one single spin for the overhand throw, with emphasis on accuracy. The tomahawk should not be thrown too hard. As in knife throwing, it is necessary to move forward or backward to determine and mark the exact distance for that perfect "stick." If properly embedded in the wood, the tomahawk handle should point downward at a 45-degree angle away from the vertical face of the target.

19. Classic Bowie knife design.

Uses of the Bowie knife

The art of tomahawk throwing is so closely tied to knife throwing that the thrower can hardly get involved with the one without becoming extremely interested in the other. Of all the knives designed through the ages, the classic Bowie pattern is perhaps the most closely akin to the weight and balance of a tomahawk. Its perfection as an all-purpose, close combat weapon has been proved in a century-and-a-half of use (Fig. 19). It can be used for chopping, thrusting, and slashing, as well as for throwing. The same can be said for the tomahawk.

20. Gurkha knife (*top*), Bowie knife (*bottom*).

Comparison of Bowie and Gurkha knives

The classic Bowie knife lends itself especially well to the "hatchet throw" because of its long, heavy, and clipped-point blade combined with a comparatively light handle. Only one other well-known knife—with the exception of a professional throwing knife—is balanced and weighted in much the same way, and that is the famed *Kukri* or Gurkha knife of India. This fabulous weapon is quite similar to both a tomahawk and a large Bowie knife in its balance as a chopping instrument (Fig. 20), and is the basic tool of the Gurkhas as well as a symbol of their race.

The blade of this great combat weapon of the legendary Gurkha warriors is sharply curved downward and is therefore much more difficult to master as a throwing-knife than is a straight-bladed knife such as the Bowie. But with a balancing point at approximately dead center of the overall length, it can be, and is, thrown most expertly by the handle in the simple overhand hatchet throw, especially if hurled by a Gurkha warrior, either from foot or from horseback.

Tomahawk underhand throw

When a sportsman becomes proficient in throwing a hatchet or tomahawk overhand he can take on the challenge of the underhand throw. This requires more skill and control and a longer throwing distance for the single spin than does the overhand throw. The weight and balance of the weapon—not necessarily the speed with which it is swung forward —will determine the rate of spin when hurled.

Your grip should be taken at the end of the handle with the butt fitted firmly and squarely against the palm of your hand. The cutting edge is pointed toward the target, and the tomahawk, hand, and forearm are lined up as straight as possible. The top knuckle of your first finger should be to the front if you are gripping the handle correctly.

Take your stance with the left foot forward, knees slightly bent, and swing the weapon back and forth a few times in the direction of your target in order to get the tomahawk lined up. Then bring it back until your right arm is about parallel to the ground and swing it down and forward smoothly in a full, underhand sweep, releasing the handle at the exact moment you feel you are lined up with your mark. A slight flip of the wrist as you make the release will control the spin. Continue to follow through on the upswing after the weapon has left your hand, because the follow-through is still the secret of achieving accuracy with both knife and tomahawk.

Knife "underhand flip"

To throw a knife underhand with the "underhand flip," as it is called, use a long, heavy-bladed weapon which will give you much better control for this type of throw than will a lightweight knife. This style of throwing requires considerable skill and much practice to achieve proficiency. Control depends on the degree of speed and the amount of spin you impart to the blade as it flips from your hand. Actually, it is more a fast "toss" than a "throw," somewhat similar to pitching horseshoes.

The knife is gripped by the handle or blade in the exact manner described previously for the overhand knife throw. The thumb is kept uppermost since the knife should always be thrown underhand with the plane of the blade horizontal. The throw is made using the same stance and swing as with the underhand tomahawk throw, holding the knife in a straight line with the wrist and forearm.

Depending on the distance, the knife can be so controlled as to make a half turn, full turn, or even $1\frac{1}{2}$ turns to stick point first. A slight flip as it leaves your hand will control the spin, but you will need considerable practice for each type of throw before you find the correct distance to stand and still retain maximum control.

At short distances, the knife can be "rifled" forward without any flip or spin to fly straight to the target, but for sporting purposes you should stand at least 15 feet from the mark and try for either a half or full spin with the underhand flip. You will find that you can successfully toss the knife for a half spin at about the same distance required for the overhand full spin. Here, again, perfect timing, control, and rhythm are necessary if you are to master this style of throwing. The similarity in techniques will be obvious to you when you compare tomahawk and knife throwing in the underhand throw.

The rate of spin is much slower using the underhand method with both knife and tomahawk than it is when throwing either weapon overhand, but the underhand style provides an excellent opportunity to sharpen your skill and adds novelty to any throwing session.

VII

SAFETY MEASURES, RULES, AND CARE OF KNIVES

In any competitive sport, it is important to operate under a set of rules or guidelines that will also include adequate safety measures.

The safety element is especially needed while throwing an edged or pointed weapon such as a knife or tomahawk, for the most obvious of reasons. Any weapon is dangerous if improperly used, and every precaution must be considered so that no accidents, however slight, will occur.

Choose a safe location

When you have constructed your target, you should make certain that it is placed in an open area with good visibility in all directions so that there is not the least chance of anyone walking up on you unobserved and maybe getting nicked with a bouncing blade.

55

You will find that when you start throwing your knives in the back yard, you may quickly attract every child in the neighborhood and possibly quite a few adults. These people could, without warning, constitute a fairly large audience. The element of danger to spectators could become very real, to the extent that you might have to use the clothes-line to rope off an area well back of your throwing position, thus keeping your friends out of harm's way!

Knives, when improperly thrown, even by an expert, can take some wild and crazy bounces in every imaginable direction. Occasionally they even bounce back toward the thrower or fly backwards over his head,—not often, but it does happen! So remember always to play it safe. Don't ever take a chance of injuring someone accidentally. Always keep both spectators and contestants well behind the knife thrower.

In contests when throwers are taking turns to determine their skill, the excitement generated by the competition can sometimes cause crowding too close to the throwing line. Therefore, it is especially important in knife or tomahawk matches to rigidly enforce safety rules and even to stop the action completely until all spectators are safely back from the throwing area.

Knife and tomahawk competitions

The rules for competition can be drawn to suit the occasion. Depending on the number of contestants, the time allotted to each thrower can be changed.

The following are some suggested rules for competition that have been tried and used successfully in many knife and tomahawk matches—especially when these sports were featured as part of the "Shoots" of gun clubs in Michigan and elsewhere.

KNIFE AND TOMAHAWK COMPETITION RULES

1. The distance to be thrown should be not less than 12 feet from the target face—the minimum distance for one full spin.
2. Three "free" practice throws are allowed to determine the range or distance for each individual contestant.
3. Hang the target, using the "Big Bull" target (the official 50-yard, slow fire pistol-target of the National Rifle Association), or the 12-inch NRA official 100-yard small bore rifle target, one target only to a contestant.
4. Score after five throws into the target, with full points counted for the highest ring that has been cut by the blade of the knife or tomahawk.
5. In case of ties, a "sudden death" contest is held, consisting of one throw at the 10X ring center, with first, second, and third places determined by the best score. (As an alternative, with only a few contestants and sufficient time available, the original contest rules may be followed over again with the full five throws.)

If official shooting targets are unavailable and not too many throwers are competing, the following rules are suggested:

KNIFE THROWING RULES WITHOUT
OFFICIAL TARGETS

1. The distance to be thrown should be not less than 12 feet from the target face—the minimum distance for one full spin.
2. Three "free" practice throws are allowed to determine the range or distance for each contestant.
3. Each contestant is allowed seven consecutive throws, of which five must stick firmly to qualify for the finals.
4. "Finals" contestants will then throw the knife 21 times; or if time is limited because of a large number of entries, this can be changed to 14 or even 7 throws in succession. The top three contestants with the most "sticks" in the series thrown will be declared the winners.
5. In case of a tie, a "sudden death" contest will be held, with each contestant making one throw only at the center of the target and at a mark approximately the size of a small coin. The thrower closest to the center of this mark is declared the winner, and the second- and third-place winners would be the next two contestants closest to the mark.

6. The size of the target face can be agreed upon in advance, or if the butt end of a sawed log is used, there need be no target face at all, with only "sticks" in the wood counting for the score.

TOMAHAWK THROWING CONTEST RULES

1. The distance to be thrown should be not less than 12 feet from the target face—the minimum distance for one full spin. (A cross-section of a large sawed log should be used for the tomahawk target if possible.)
2. Three "free" practice throws are allowed to determine range or distance for each individual contestant.
3. Each contestant is allowed seven consecutive throws, of which five must stick firmly to qualify for the semi-finals.
4. In the semi-finals each contestant is allowed four throws only and, to qualify for the finals, must stick his tomahawk in each of the four quadrants of a 20-inch circular target face which is quartered by cross tapes, or cross lines.
5. In tomahawk finals, only one throw is allowed. The winner is decided by the throw closest to the center of the crossed tapes, measuring from the center of the tomahawk edge to the center of the crossed tapes. Second and third places would go to the next two contestants placing tomahawks closest to the center of the crossed tapes.

The above rules can be modified to suit the occasion. Thus, the mark or bull's-eye can be any sized circle that the contestants may agree upon, with paper plates or circular disks cut from cardboard providing simple but effective target faces. Permanent bull's-eyes can be painted on the wood or sprayed on with an aerosol paint, using a standard size coffee can open at both ends to make a perfect circle for the mark.

If there are enough true "experts" competing with knife or tomahawk, they can step back and hold their own contest, throwing a double or even triple spin instead of sticking to the conventional one-spin distance.

Knife-throwing clubs

Knife-throwing groups can be organized into clubs or associations, with officers and committees elected or appointed to arrange for competitions. Contests may include novelty events such as balloon breaking, throwing at animal target faces, or even throwing at moving targets with knife or tomahawk. Trick knife throwing can be demonstrated, such as underhand throwing, throwing between the legs, throwing backward underhanded, or lying on your back with your head towards the target and flipping the blades over your head. Fast-draw throwing and other stunts can be incorporated into competitive events to add considerable interest and novelty to the occasion.

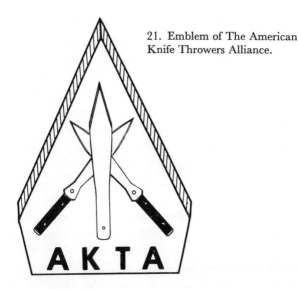

21. Emblem of The American Knife Throwers Alliance.

American Knife Throwers Alliance

For knife-throwing enthusiasts there is also a national organization that they can join. It is The American Knife Throwers Alliance, an association of American sportsmen dedicated to the practice and promotion of knife throwing as a sport, recreation, and hobby. The organization was founded by the author in the spring of 1971 to provide guidelines for competition in the sport, to help local groups organize into clubs, and to serve as a clearing house for information concerning knives and knife throwing in general. The principal means of communication between all AKTA members and their national headquarters in Grand Rapids, Michigan, is via a quarterly newsletter, *The Bullseye Buster,* plus personal correspondence between members (Fig. 21).

Competition is as important to knife-throwing adherents as it is to other sports. It is planned to hold regional and national contests under the sponsorship and encouragement of The American Knife Throwers Alliance whenever and wherever sufficient interest and local support is indicated.

Knife care

Care of knives is most important. The same attention should be given to them as you would devote to your gun or bow. The blades should be cleaned with a mild household detergent, rinsed, and wiped dry. Silicone-impregnated cloth and paper toweling are fine for wiping the knives. If you do not plan to use them for a few days or longer, you should oil them lightly to prevent rust.

A fine-grained file can be used to smooth out slight nicks in the handle slabs or on the blade, and the handles can also be touched up and smoothed with fine sandpaper. The points should be kept sharp with a file. Finally, the weapons should be stored in a dry place out of reach of small boys. After all, you want them to grow up to become knife throwers too.

VIII

THE PROFESSIONALS

The glamour, showmanship, and drama inherent in the art of knife throwing are provided by the professionals. They are a small group of talented performers who create the image of the art. They provide the inspiration to those sportsmen knife throwers who may never want to become professionals, but who envy and admire them for their skill and style in throwing knives.

Professional throwing style

The truly great professionals in any given era of time are few in number. Each one has a style of throwing and a matched set of knives uniquely his own. In most cases the professional has either designed his own knives or inherited them from his father or some other predecessor who was a noted professional in his time.

22. Professional throwing-knife.

Since a professional normally uses only one set of knives for the various phases or stunts of his act, the basic design may vary from 12 to 16 inches overall, with the balancing point at approximately the dead center of the overall length. The forward part of the knife is usually a wide, symmetrical diamond or leaf-shaped design, or, in some cases, it has the classic Bowie point with a curved cutting edge and a clipped top. The handle half of the weapon is tapered to fit the hand comfortably (Fig. 22).

This knife is primarily designed to throw by the handle. But because the balancing point is exactly at the overall center and there are no sharp edges to cut the hand, it can also be thrown with force and accuracy when gripped by the blade and thrown handle first. However, because of his flat-footed stance, which is somewhat different from that of the sportsman knife thrower, the professional always throws his knife with the plane of the blade *vertical*, regardless of whether he hurls it by the handle or the blade. The reason is that his knives must always thud into the wood in close proximity to his live "target" and in vertical alignment with the target boards themselves for maximum penetration and elimination of added risk.

Most professionals use a long knife for several reasons. One is that it is more flashy and awe-inspiring under the bright spotlights. Another is that the longer knife, up to approximately 16 inches in length, can give them better control. And, finally, a long knife has the weight needed for maximum penetration. It will remain "stuck" after it strikes the exact spot at which it was thrown, and will not be jarred loose by the impact of the other blades.

Knives used by professionals do not have cross-pieces, guards, or hilts such as are found in fighting knives where a crosspiece of brass or steel is desirable to guard the hand against the cutting stroke of an opponent. A crosspiece in a knife designed for professional use would be dangerous to that pretty girl standing against the target. A thrown knife might possibly bounce off the protruding guard of a previously embedded knife and cause serious injury.

The professional knife has nothing to break the symmetry of its lines from the point to the end of the handle. Either there are no handle slabs at all, or else the handle is merely taped. Many professionals prefer to use plain white adhesive tape on knife handles, since white shows up especially well under the spotlights. A crosspiece, in addition to adding a risk to the act, could also upset the delicate balance of the knife itself and cause an imperfect throw. A throwing-knife intended for sporting use only can have a small guard separating the handle from the blade; but to a professional this feature is not desirable since it is mostly ornamental.

Stance and throwing technique

There is very little difference between a professional throwing-knife and the handle-throwing type used by the sportsman knife thrower. There is, however, quite a difference in the stance and in the throwing techniques used by each group. Figure 23 illustrates the basic similarities of knives used by professionals and the professional types widely used by sportsmen.

The wind-up, normally used by the sportsman knife thrower, is all but eliminated by the professional. This puts him up to five feet closer to the target. He starts his throw, providing he is right-handed, with a flat-footed stance. His left foot is forward and his knees are slightly bent in a half crouch. The ball of his left foot, upon which he puts his weight when he throws, provides most of the balance and stability required. As the result of many years of almost daily practice, that throw is flawless. His follow-through and accuracy are both perfect, and it is that consistent accuracy that distinguishes the professional from the sportsman knife thrower.

It has been pointed out that since knives used by professionals have no sharp edges to cut the hand,

23. Professional throwing-knives (*left to right*): sportsman's model throwing-knife; special model used by author; professional model; professional knife thrown by Kenneth L. Pierce; professional knife thrown by Paul LaCross.

they always throw their knives with the plane of the blade vertical, regardless of whether it is hurled by handle or blade. This gives them a consistency of performance at all normal distances, including the half spin, full spin, and the one-and-one-half spin. Their stance and throwing movements remain the same for every throw, with only the distance to their target adjusted for the type of throw executed.

24. Handle grip for professional throwing.

Professionals have one special advantage over the sportsman knife thrower: years of practice and training enable them accurately to judge the exact distance needed from their target to make each knife stick perfectly.

Some good, professional advice for the sportsman to consider is that the $1\frac{1}{2}$ spin—when thrown by the blade and in the professional style—is the most accurate throw he can adopt. He can usually achieve better control than is possible with the handle throw because the wide part of the blade fills his hand better and adds more stability to the throw.

This advice would be especially valuable to the thrower who not only has mastered the professional style of hurling his blades but also uses a true professional knife of the design shown in Figure 22.

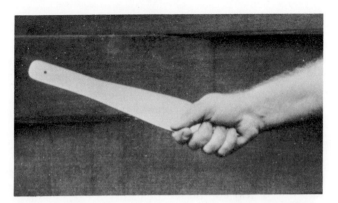

25. Blade grip for professional throwing.

With the balancing point at approximately the exact center of the knife, either the handle throw or the blade throw is effective (Figs. 24, 25). An experienced thrower can stick the weapon either way practically every time. But there is something about the blade grip and the way it fills your hand that is quickly appreciated by the advanced knife thrower. Professionals seem to prefer the blade grip for most of the throws performed in their acts, and their accuracy—being superb in comparison to that of a nonprofessional— certainly points to the inescapable conclusion that the professional blade throw must provide the greatest amount of accuracy! Why, otherwise, would the professionals use it?

It is a point worth pondering. Go prove it to yourself.

Great masters of the art

Some professionals throw their knives in the classic manner while others have a unique style all their own. A splendid example of this special style is demonstrated by one of the greatest professional knife throwers of the present generation—Kenneth Pierce.

The son of Lawrence Pierce—Chief White Cloud of the Seneca Indian Nation of New York State and also one of the fine professionals of an earlier era—Ken Pierce is undoubtedly the fastest knife thrower the world has ever seen (Fig. 26).

Professionally known as Prince Che-Che of the Senecas and dressed in colorful Indian garb, Mr. Pierce throws a matched set of nine knives that were designed and made by his father shortly after World War I. He hurls all nine at considerably less than one-second intervals in a criss-cross pattern for an almost skin-tight pinning of his lovely young wife, Donna—billed as Princess Shining Star—thus giving a most amazing demonstration of his lightning speed, accuracy, and versatility. His foot-long knives are "fanned," similar to cards from a deck, from his left hand to his right for the half-spin blade throw in such a dazzling blue of motion that the eye can hardly follow the sequence from the first to the ninth knife.

Unlike other professional knife throwers who build a vertical "ladder" around their target one

26. Kenneth L. Pierce—Prince Che Che—who is known as the world's fastest knife thrower.

blade at a time in a clockwise or counter-clockwise rotation, Che-Che's uncanny speed and dexterity in throwing accurately enable him to criss-cross his knives—one to the left, one to the right—for all nine throws, until the encirclement of his "target" is completed. His distance is approximately nine feet from the board.

With the confidence of long and constant training (he started to throw professionally at the age of seven as a member of the world renowned White Cloud Troupe), Kenneth Pierce hurls his knives close to his "target" in one of the most spectacular demonstrations of speed and accuracy ever seen.

The great master of the classic style of knife throwing is Paul LaCross, who for perfect accuracy with the thrown knife has never been surpassed. Mr. LaCross is widely acclaimed, and rightly so, by millions of people who have witnessed his performances on television and in personal appearances as "The World's Fastest, Fanciest Gunslinger, Knife and Tomahawk Thrower."

Considered by experts to be perhaps the finest and fastest trick shot artist with revolvers and rifles in this modern age, Paul LaCross is no less famous around the world for his knife and tomahawk throwing skills. With probably the quickest reflexes in show business in the art of the fast draw, he nevertheless throws his knives in a slightly more painstaking manner and seldom, if ever, makes a mistake. When that 16-inch blade leaves his hand it hits exactly where he aimed it! His accuracy with guns has been carried over into his knife and tomahawk throwing skills, resulting in the most flawless throwing technique ever achieved by a classic-style professional knife thrower.

Since Mr. LaCross is left-handed and completely ambidextrous with his revolver marksmanship, his left-handed style of throwing knives and tomahawks adds an interest to his technique never completely matched by a right-hander. He throws both single and half spins during his performance, and his accuracy at the longer distance is fully as perfect as it is with just the half spin (Figs. 27–30).

The one thing that all professionals have in common despite their individual throwing styles is that they all had to learn their skill the same way.

"When I first started to throw knives professionally at the age of seven, I had already received two years of training from my father," Kenneth Pierce remarked. "As a boy only five years old, my education as a knife thrower began. To learn to throw professionally it is necessary to train daily for long hours and for months on end. When you become good enough to use a live target, you first throw the knives wide until your confidence begins to build. As you get more confident, you move each knife in closer to the live target until finally you always know just exactly where each knife will stick. When that time comes, you are ready to perform before an audience. The process of learning and training can take years."

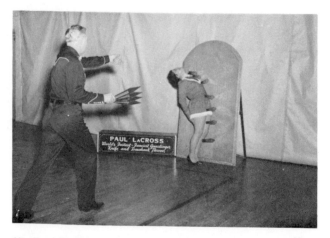

27. Paul LaCross in a knife-throwing demonstration with his wife.

28. Cutting paper while throwing backwards.

29. Outlining Mrs. LaCross while throwing blindfolded.

30. Paul LaCross throwing his knives on both sides of his daughter, Paula, on "The Wheel of Death."

Special throws

Almost every professional knife thrower has his own particular "bag of tricks"—certain stunts in which he may specialize and which are not necessarily performed by other members of the profession. There are also certain standard "throws" with a knife that are intended to do specific things for the professional. Kenneth Pierce lists four that he uses in various parts of his act:

1. STRAIGHT KNIFE: used to hit the target squarely and straight in;
2. DROP KNIFE: used for a skin-tight throw with the handle down;
3. RAISE KNIFE: used for a skin-tight throw with the handle up;
4. POWER KNIFE: thrown with full power straight in, for speed and maximum penetration of the wood.

All professionals use these same types of throws, or at least can use them, but the simple "straight knife" throw is the one normally demonstrated.

The Wheel of Death

The most popular stunt among the professionals is called, quite dramatically, "The Wheel of Death." A colorful circular target, approximately six feet in diameter and two or more inches thick, is mounted on a stand with ball-bearing arrangement in the center that permits the target to revolve rapidly. The assistant stands on a small platform with hand grips at her sides and sometimes straps to keep her in position while the wheel is spinning. The wheel used by Paul LaCross spins at a rate of 120 r.p.m. while he throws knives on both sides of his daughter Paula, six to a side. This takes split-second timing and a remarkable eye, but never—never—does he make a mistake! The identical stunt is also performed by Kenneth Pierce.

Another great professional, Joe Gibson, has performed this act for years, throwing with a hood over his head. He has—so the story goes—been able to see a "little," but has mainly relied on a device that clicks audibly on the revolving target every time it passes the vertical position. Primarily it is a matter of precise and accurate timing of the throw.

Mouth-held objects as targets

Cutting paper strips held horizontally in the mouth of the assistant is another good, standard professional stunt. In some cases even fresh flowers are used, with daisies, dahlias, and tulips among those considered most suitable for this act. The assistant usually stands a bit forward of the target board so that the edge of the knife cuts the object she holds between her lips. Paul LaCross has often done this stunt the hard way—throwing backwards and sometimes even sighting his target through a mirror.

Throwing blindfolded

A thrill is always provided for the audience when the professional performs blindfolded. Perhaps some can see a "little" through the hood or blindfold, thus reducing the risk but retaining the dramatic effect. Paul LaCross, however, does it with a double blindfold that he *cannot* see through. In describing this great act, he wrote the author:

On the blindfold stunt I do it by sound only. I use a double blindfold, and we let someone from the audience carefully examine it to prove that I cannot see through it. After my assistant puts the blindfold on me she also places a black bag over my head which comes down below my neck so as to make certain that I cannot see over the top or underneath the blindfold covering my eyes.

She gives me the set of knives—all but one, which she keeps in her hand. She then turns me around and faces me toward the knife board. Then she goes back and stands against the center of the board, facing me. With the knife she has retained from the set, she proceeds to tap the knife board, indicating to me by sound only just where I am to stick the knife. She continues to tap the board before each throw until the last knife is thrown and her body is closely encircled by the blades.

Another stunt he does well is throwing two knives at once, so that in six throws his assistant is neatly outlined by twelve blades.

Throwing at a screened human target

One of the major demonstrations of skill performed by most professionals is outlining the assistant with knives that are hurled through a large paper screen or curtain which, in most cases, is bent loosely around her and thumbtacked to the back of the target board.

There are two basic techniques that have been used by many generations of professional knife throwers in performing this stunt. In one, the professional throws his knives into an imaginary, vertical line an exact distance from the edge of the target on each side, which gives his assistant an adequate safety margin. In the other, the hidden assistant shifts her body balance from one leg to the other so as to leave as wide a space as possible between herself and each vertical ladder of blades.

Since this act is always well rehearsed and prearranged as to which side of the target the knives will be hurled into first, the assistant knows just where each blade will stick—six knives on her right, starting near the feet and working up, then six knives on her left, for example.

Although she is hidden by the screen, generally made of pasted-up newspapers or colored paper, the assistant usually has her feet and ankles exposed to the audience and, of course, to the knife thrower himself, so that everyone will know she is really there while the knives are being thrown.

Since the assistant can move her body sideways from six to eight inches without otherwise moving her feet, the professional has what is to him a good wide area in which to throw around her in a most dramatic manner. While an element of risk is always present, the stunt looks a lot more dangerous than it really is when performed this way.

Paul LaCross explains

This particular demonstration, along with "The Wheel of Death" and throwing while completely blindfolded, can, however, really be turned into a most dangerous and thrilling spectacle. Paul LaCross has made it so with his own version of the act, which he described in his own words:

> In my case, I use either a plain white bed sheet or a piece of unmarked white paper six feet wide by seven feet long. Instead of having it wrapped around my assistant and thumb-tacked to the board, I use an aluminum rod in both ends of the curtain or screen. It is rolled up on one rod and attached to the other. Grasping one rod as close to the center as possible, my assistant lifts it high above her head, unrolling the screen upward from the bottom rod which rests on the floor in front of the target.

Now the curtain is *not* wrapped around her but instead is straight across in front of her body, thus hiding her outline completely. It is as if she were standing behind a wall and having knives thrown around her through the wall and sticking into the knife board behind her. Since the knife board which she stands in front of is only three feet in width and the curtain itself is six feet wide and reaches from the floor to high above her head, the assistant is completely hidden, including her feet.

There are no markings whatsoever on the paper screen, and when throwing the knives around her I do it completely by judgment—estimating how far over the edge of the board the curtain extends and how far in from the edge of the screen is her body. I proceed to throw the knives in rapid succession, starting on the left side and working up from legs to head, and then repeating the process on the right side, with only my judgment to guide me as to where each knife is to be thrown.

When the last blade is hurled, I run up and pull the curtain away from her, exposing her body encircled by the thrown knives. This is more spectacular than if her feet or outline behind the screen were visible; and since no one sees my assistant during the entire throwing sequence, the act becomes more daring and exciting to the audience.

Some impalement acts used by other knife-throwing professionals have been a little too spectacular. Joe Gibson is said once to have used big, two-pound hatchets in a stunt in which he hurled them around his wife, Hannah. But Mrs. Gibson, noting the audience reaction, detected fear and horror in the faces of some of the spectators, and the stunt was scrubbed from the act. The same has been true in spear-hurling sequences demonstrated in other impalement acts. Some stunts simply appear too dangerous to achieve favorable public acceptance.

Knives of fire

Flaming knives always add great interest to a knife-throwing act. The handles are specially wrapped and soaked with kerosene or other flammable material. The blades are gripped by the point and thrown handle first after being ignited. If the act is performed in a partial blackout, the spinning fire knives are quite spectacular. The stunt is not done too often because of fire regulations; and if demonstrated in the open air, even a slight breeze could make things a bit warm for the unfortunate assistant.

Many other knife-throwing stunts have been perfected and demonstrated through the ages, but those mentioned herein are the ones most often performed by modern professionals.

While tribute is due to the fine skill and technique of the professional knife throwers themselves, it must be remembered that they are part of a team. That charming lady who braves the dangers of a slightly miscalculated throw should come in for her share of the glory and glamour that are part of the aura or essence of the act. As it takes "two to tango," so it also takes two people to provide a professional knife-throwing performance.

Lovely and brave ladies, like Mrs. Paul La Cross and daughter Paula, and Donna Pierce, not only supply the necessary touch of beauty but also provide the coolness and skill as living "targets" that inspire the professional himself to make each performance a memorable one for the audience.

Sportsmen knife throwers can also learn the "tricks of the trade" if they want to quit their jobs and take up the profession as a full-time occupation. On the other hand, one great professional, Frank Dean, along with his assistant and wife, Bernice, retired in the late 1930s and started a thriving mail order business making and selling throwing-knives and distributing an interesting booklet he wrote entitled, "The Art of Knife Throwing." Mr. Dean provided much of the knife-throwing action seen in motion pictures of the period, working with some of his excellent contemporaries in the "art of impalement," such as Bennie Pete, Jack Cavanaugh, Frank Chicarello, and Steve Clemento.

So, to the professionals of the past, as well as to those of today and even tomorrow, the modern knife-throwing sportsman owes his respect and genuine admiration.

One final point to consider: If you master the professional style of throwing, it may give you a slight edge in achieving "pin-point" accuracy over the "sportsman style" of knife throwing.

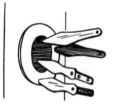

HUNTING: A NEW TWIST
TO AN OLD SPORT

As the sport of knife throwing continues to grow, and more and more sportsmen take up this fascinating recreation, so grows their natural interest in the possibilities of the throwing-knife as a hunting weapon.

Killing game with a knife designed expressly for throwing has been accomplished on occasion by a small handful of sportsmen knife throwers, but far too few can really claim any measure of success. There are practically no records available to indicate where and when kills have been made and what type of small game has been bagged with a throwing-knife. Also, there have been no known or publicized kills thus far of big game such as deer. Surely a feat such as bringing down a deer with a thrown knife would have made the news media from coast to coast.

As already noted, almost anyone can learn to throw a knife with skill and accuracy if he practices with the weapon long and hard. But in hunting game there are two additional stumbling blocks in the path of success, even for an expert knife thrower. These are stalking and throwing at an unknown distance from the prey.

Stalking

Guns, arrows, spears, darts, and even boomerangs can bring down game at fairly long range, but it is only by the art of skillful stalking that the knife thrower can get close enough to make his throw, no matter how good or bad that throw might be. Most knife throwers have also had experience in hunting with gun or bow and, therefore, must have learned some of the fundamentals of how to stalk.

Numerous good books and magazine articles have been written about hunting, and in practically every one the art of stalking is recognized as an important part of each successful hunt.

One of the best definitions of stalking was written by Stanley E. Brock, noted writer, hunter, and sportsman, and for many years a professional hunter and rancher in the remote savannahs of the border country between Guyana and northern Brazil. In his book, *Hunting in the Wilderness* (Hale, London, 1963), Mr. Brock wrote: "Stalking is the art of approaching an already spied animal to within shooting range." Substitute "throwing-knife" for the word "shooting," and you have the perfect definition—short, and to the point.

Since Mr. Brock has been seen and heard by millions as one of the stars of the television series "Wild Kingdom," one tends to forget that even before his TV debut Stan Brock was considered to be one of the most expert stalkers in the world—and he still is today.

Stalking is an art that requires considerable practice alone in the woods, jungle, or wherever the hunted game happens to be. Any hunter knows his chances are better for getting within shooting range if he can approach his quarry from down wind. This is because human scent is more alarming to a wild animal than is any other kind of disturbance. Knowledge of the movements and habits of the animal you are stalking is also of great importance. Best of all is experience, which you can only get by actually stalking.

It is probably wisest to start with small game such as rabbits, squirrels, groundhogs, or whatever small animals are available and convenient for you to practice on. Stalking skills are not too critical in this phase of hunting; but if you ever go after bigger game with a throwing-knife, you had better know exactly what you are doing. If your stalking abilities are limited and yet you want to try getting close enough for a throw at big game, you can use a blind or a platform up in a tree above a game trail. Both methods are widely employed for conventional deer hunting, and there is no reason they should not prove suitable for use by a knife thrower.

It isn't going to be easy, but it is quite possible that big game kills with a throwing-knife will yet be made from blinds or tree platforms. Of these two, the tree platform above a game trail is most recommended. (Make sure to check hunting laws in your area first.)

Hunting weapons

A sharp-edged, heavy-bladed knife such as the Bowie-Axe throwing-knife (Fig. 31) is recommended for the type of hunting where you take to the trees. To stop or knock over big game, a hunter needs a weapon with a lot of shocking power. A lightweight knife is not likely to accomplish this on anything larger than a rabbit. For big game you need sharp cutting edges combined with a foot or more of length and nearly a full pound of cold steel to get effective penetration and the necessary shocking wallop! The handle-throwing type is best suited for this purpose.

In the opinion of two experts at hunting small game with the throwing-knife—P. D. Malone, of Boston, and Ted David, of Muskogee, Oklahoma— a good-sized knife with sharp point and edges is most important. Mr. Malone is primarily a varment hunter with throwing-knives and has killed many types of small game as well as numerous poisonous snakes in the swamps of the American South.

31. Bowie-axe throwing-knife.

"Ground squirrels and rabbits, along with the snakes, make excellent targets for the knife-throwing hunter," he wrote the author. "Porcupines, raccoons, frogs, weasels, muskrats, and woodchucks also make good, easy targets if the knife hunter wants to go after them."

A hunting experience

Dr. David, an avid hunter and knife thrower, also wrote to the author about the first reported throwing-knife kill of fairly large game in March of 1968:

> I packed up my equipment and took off for our camp in the swamps of Florida. We do our hunting of deer, turkey, duck, pig, coon, and occasionally a bear, in some sections we lease by the year. I knew the easiest game to try first would be the pig. We have quite a few year-around litters, and I could pick the size. Besides being good eating, the 25- to 40-pound wild pig is relatively easy to stalk, with a lot of quiet and patience.

During the two days we hunted I apparently proved how humans cannot always relate to experience. Using a special 13-ounce throwing-knife I had a hit on a small 30-pound pig. Probably it was just behind the ribs, and here is the point I should have realized: there was not enough shock to stop it or to impede its flight. We did not have a dog with us and soon lost its trail in the swamp. The next pig I hit was with the Bowie-Axe knife, which weighs about one pound, and the difference was most noticeable. It was almost knocked over by the impact, moved away much more slowly, and was easily found about 150 yards from the impact point. The knife had pierced the left chest cavity and abdomen at the diaphragm and was still embedded.

We found the first pig the next day—dead—with the aid of dogs. It had run over one quarter mile before dropping, and the knife had been dislodged and was lost.

Dr. David also explained that his experience in these two hunting incidents clearly pointed up the need for adequate shocking power. The heavier of the two throwing-knives did a more efficient job of bringing down his quarry, a Florida 40-pound wild pig, which has almost unbelievable strength and stamina.

32. Peter S. LaGana and his fighting tomahawk.

Tomahawk hunting

Knife throwers in increasing numbers are also attempting to take wild game with the tomahawk. One very successful tomahawk hunter is Peter S. La Gana, of Ebensburg, Pennsylvania, the designer of a beautiful combination fighting and throwing tomahawk (Fig. 32).

For hunting groundhogs and similar-sized animals, he throws with a side-arm motion, as if hurling a boomerang, and has been quite successful in bagging such game. For target-throwing, however, he uses the conventional overhand tomahawk throw.

Special weapons and techniques

In addition to the need for a proper knife and experience in stalking, a skilled knife thrower is also confronted with the problem of sticking his quarry while throwing at an unknown distance. There is no easy solution to this problem, although one very noted "old timer" in the art of bagging small game, Jim Ramsey, of Lincoln, New Mexico, has designed and made a number of interesting throwing weapons with at least four sticking points that work well for him. These are mostly variations of all-metal tomahawk types with sticking points at each end of the handle and on the front and back ends of the blade itself (Figs. 33, 34).

However, the average knife thrower must usually trust to luck and hope that his knife will strike his quarry point first if he is throwing at an unknown distance. The secret is to hurl the weapon hard and fast. There is at least one chance in eight that it will hit point first. With a heavy enough throwing-knife the impact will probably stun or knock over the game if struck even with a butt-end or sideways wallop of the weapon. In that case, it might be possible to get off a second throw with that spare throwing-knife the hunter should always carry.

Hunting knives

Difficult as it may seem to stick game properly while throwing at an unknown distance, there is

33, 34. Jim Ramsey, with some of his multiple-pointed throwing weapons.

35. Throwing knives designed for use in hunting game.

still one simple method that will at least reduce the guesswork. No doubt you have already thought of it yourself—and you are right. Get a throwing-knife with a point on both ends. This can be a simple but very effective "game-getter" or "varmint-sticker," or whatever name you choose to give this weapon. The main thing is that it be balanced in the center with enough weight to provide shocking power and of sufficient length to give the thrower maximum control. You could even throw a steel rod pointed at both ends, although genuine sporting types of throwing-knives used for hunting are still true knives and not gadgets.

Some good, tried, and proven knives for hunting

game are shown in Figure 35. Sometimes a knife thrower will have a series of small holes drilled in his blade about $\frac{3}{4}$ of an inch apart. The theory is that when the weapon is hurled at the quarry, the wind will be forced through these holes and the rapidly spinning blade will emit a faint, pulsating, whistle-like sound that should inspire the critter to pause and listen, thus sealing its doom!

The hunting of game with a modern throwing-knife is a new and challenging idea. But to any hunter worthy of the name who accepts that challenge, the sport can offer wider horizons and an exciting new field of recreation. Perhaps even a rabbit stew!

X

TALES, LEGENDS, AND PEOPLE

There are many tales and traditional yarns about knives and edged weapons in general, but few indeed about knife throwing or throwing-knives specifically. The original knife carried by Col. James Bowie, who became a legend in his own lifetime, is the one blade in American history that became legendary. It survived some notorious duels and close-quarter fighting in which Jim Bowie was involved, only to disappear, perhaps forever, at his dramatic death in the Alamo.

The Bowie knife

This type of knife was thrown countless times from the 1830s through the American Civil War era. Almost every frontiersman of that time in history and many "gentlemen," including members of Congress, felt undressed without a Bowie knife on their hips. As a close combat weapon it was without peer, and it was also a first-rate throwing-knife of the period. Extremely popular among Confederate soldiers, especially during the first half of the Civil War, it provided the means for knife throwing as a form of recreation to enliven camp life.

Resurgence of knife throwing

One hundred years is a long time for a sport to wait for "rebirth," but apparently it took that long for the resurgence of the sport as we see it today.

Some research into the annals of history has uncovered a most interesting line drawing entitled "Camp Life in the Confederate Army—Mississippians Practicing with the Bowie Knife." This drawing first appeared on page 556 of the August 31, 1861 issue of the old *Harper's Weekly*, when the Civil War had just begun and Confederate hopes were high. The artist could hardly have just imagined all that interest shown by the "Rebs" in throwing their Bowie knives at a mark on a large tree, but his concept of what those Bowie knives really looked like leaves much to be desired. The drawing is important, however, because it proves that knife throwing was popular, especially among the "Bowie-totin'" Southerners, as far back as 1861.

If other legends about knife throwing ever develop, it will probably be because of events to take place in the future, if certain plans of a somewhat wistful nature come to pass. One talented Michigan knife thrower has expressed a desire to try his skill with a throwing-knife—and his luck—on a Michigan black bear (supported by a friend or two armed with 30.06-deer rifles, just in case). Another knife thrower, who is a nationally known ski expert from Oregon, has told of his hopes to pursue and overtake some large game animal—perhaps even an elk—while skiing across the snow, and to bring down his quarry with a thrown blade. Of such schemes are tales and legends born.

Stories are also told of combat knives or short bayonets thrown successfully in battle during desperate situations. Motion pictures and television programs are full of such incidents that have been fictionalized. Manufacturers of modern hunting, combat, and throwing-knives have impressive files of letters from customers describing some of the uses to which these knives have been put—some humorous, some grim, and some deadly.

Every throwing-knife that is sold is put to some use by its buyer, even if only to grace a wall or go into a collection. With the modern sport of knife throwing expanding each year at an accelerating rate, there is little doubt that before long there will be tales and legends galore of throwing-knives and of the men who hurl them, whether it be for hunting, recreation, or as a profession.

Growth of the sport has been encouraged and supported by the efforts of practically every sportsman knife-thrower. Cutlery manufacturers and dealers who may themselves be knife throwers have done wonders to interest other sportsmen everywhere. Professional knife throwers such as Frank Dean, Kenneth Pierce, and Paul LaCross have laid aside their professional mantles to step down and show sportsmen how they, too, can learn to throw a knife.

Famous craftsmen and throwers

There are a number of fine sportsmen who have done much to bring the sport of knife throwing into the spotlight it deserves. Just a few of the people who have made significant contributions to the present status of the sport include:

WILLIAM SCAGEL. The late William Scagel of Muskegon, Michigan, passed away in March 1963, after a full life of 90 years, during which he was noted as the greatest American knife crafter of the first half of the 20th century. He made many knives for the famous expeditions of the Smithsonian Institution, and Scagel knives were true "artistry in steel" (Fig. 36). Among the thousands of beautiful, edged weapons he created were, of course, a small number of throwing-knives. His blades today are practically legendary collector's items and of considerable value.

THE RANDALLS. One of the most significant results of "Old Bill" Scagel's knife craftsmanship was the

36. A collection of Scagel knives.

inspiration it gave to W. D. Randall, who, because of a Scagel knife and Scagel's early encouragement, started on the road to cutlery fame in the mid-1930s as the maker of the famous Randall-Made knives.

Following in the footsteps of William Scagel was W. D. Randall, widely known as "Bo," of Orlando, Florida. "Knife Maker Unexcelled" is a proper description of Bo Randall, and it also applies to his son, Gary, who, like his father, is a creative genius with cutlery. Combat troops of three major wars have worn Randall-Made knives into battle, and Randall knives were the first in space, carried by America's first group of astronauts through many orbits of the earth (Fig. 37).

37. W. D. "Bo" Randall and his son, Gary.

A talented knife thrower himself, Bo Randall, along with the Corrado brothers of Chicago, was the first major cutlery dealer in America to recognize the growing interest in knife throwing among sportsmen and to provide them with the best professional type of throwing-knives designed and handcrafted by American knife makers.

THE CORRADOS. The celebrated knife house of Corrado Cutlery in Chicago, Illinois, is operated by Carmen Corrado and his brother, Victor. These men were the first to recognize and encourage the sale of handcrafted American knives made by the new generation of cutlery craftsmen, including Bo Randall, Gil Hibben, H. H. Buck, Alfred Buck, and the author. Carmen Corrado developed an early interest in throwing knives as a sales specialty following his return from World War II.

His brother, Victor, also became interested, and through their combined efforts the Corrado brothers now sell throwing-knives of modern design made by American throwing-knife craftsmen as well as those imported from Europe and elsewhere. They have brought the instruments of the art to sportsmen knife throwers throughout the United States and in many foreign countries (Fig. 38).

CHARLES GRUZANSKI. The first major effort to organize the sport of knife throwing and to establish a model or blueprint for knife-throwing clubs was made by the late Charles V. Gruzanski, a police sergeant in Chicago at the time of his death in January 1972.

Formerly a professional soldier stationed for many years in Okinawa, Korea, and Japan, Chuck Gruzanski became one of the foremost American experts in judo, karate, and other systems of self-defense. While a member of the Chicago police, he organized the Tru-Flyte Knife Throwers of America in 1964 and sponsored a bimonthly publication, "The Knife-Thrower." Author of articles on self-defense in police publications and a book, *Spike and Chain—Japanese Fighting Arts* (Tuttle, 1968), Mr. Gruzanski also collaborated with the author in the production of the book *Knife Throwing as a Modern Sport* (Thomas, 1965) (Fig. 39)

38. Victor and Carmen Corrado.

39. Charles V. Gruzanski, the noted expert.

40. Dan Dannenberg, knife-thrower and craftsman.

DAN DANNENBERG. Behind every successful knife crafter there is an associate who contributed mightily to his achievement. Rex Dannenberg, known to his many friends as Dan, is the technical expert on the shaping and polishing of steel whose talents and skills in the production of fine handcrafted cutlery have helped to make the author's own TRU-BAL knives the success they are. A knife thrower of talent, Dan Dannenberg has long been associated with the production of knives. As a thrower and craftsman himself, he knows the secrets of bringing out the best in every piece of super-tough, tempered spring steel handcrafted into a throwing-knife (Fig. 40).

104 CHAPTER TEN

To HARRY McEVOY—
With Good Wishes...
J.B. Montgomery
Gen. USAF (Ret)

41. Major General (USAF ret.) J. B. Montgomery demonstrating his sport.

MAJOR GENERAL (USAF-ret.) J. B. MONTGOMERY. A distinguished military man, aerospace executive, and the former commanding general of the Eighth Air Force, Gen. Montgomery has won many contests sponsored by the Conquistadores del Cielo, a social-business group in California including approximately 100 aerospace executives. He has personally instructed numerous knife-throwing aspirants, and his enthusiasm, skill, and interest have brought many sportsmen of note into the ranks of American knife throwers. Gen. Montgomery has perhaps done more than any one person on the West Coast to promote interest and participation in knife throwing (Fig. 41).

It is, indeed, impossible to mention all the many people who have helped create interest in knife throwing. Sportsmen such as A. J. McMickle, Major R. O. Ackerman, P. D. Malone, Skillman Suydam, Danny O'Donnell, the late Dick Van Sickle, Neil Speiser, Bill Tharp, John S. Day, Samuel E. Ashmore, John Ek, Bryce Metcalf, Jack Kelchner—and many, many more—have done much to encourage the interest and participation of others in this outstanding recreational activity.

So, to knife throwers everywhere—the best of luck, good throwing, play it safe, and show the world that this is a sport in which almost anyone can enthusiastically and proudly participate.

APPENDIX:
PRACTICAL INFORMATION

At the time of publication of this book the following American firms stock and sell excellent quality throwing-knives for sportsmen knife throwers:

Tru-Balance Knife Co.,
2155 Tremont Blvd.,
N.W., Grand Rapids,
Michigan 49504

Randall-Made Knives,
P. O. Box 1988,
Orlando, Florida 32802

Corrado Cutlery, Inc.,
26 North Clark St.,
Chicago, Illinois 60602

Stoddard's,
50 Temple Place,
Boston, Mass. 02111

Paragon
Sporting Goods Co.,
871 Broadway,
New York, N. Y. 10003

San Francisco
Gun Exchange,
124 Second Street,
San Francisco,
Calif. 94105

The Exclusive
Cutlery Shop,
170 Geary Street,
San Francisco,
Calif. 94108

Deercliff
Archery Supplies,
2852 LaVista Road,
Vista Grove
Shopping Center,
Decatur, Georgia 30033

The Old Knife Shop,
Knott's Berry Farm
(Ghost Town)
Buena Park,
Calif. 90620

Hibben Knives,
P. O. Box 3914,
Anchorage, Alaska 99501

Van Sickle Knives,
P. O. Drawer 3688,
San Angelo,
Texas 76901

Williams Bros.,
566 Market Street,
San Francisco,
Calif. 94104

Casanova Guns, Inc.,
1601 W. Greenfield Ave.,
Milwaukee,
Wisconsin 53204

The Cutlery,
Eastfield Mall,
Springfield,
Mass. 01129

Olsen Knife Co., Inc.,
Howard City,
Mich. 49329

OTHER TUTTLE BOOKS

Historical and Geographical Dictionary of Japan *by E. Papinot*

A History of Japanese Literature *by W. G. Aston*

I Am a Cat *by Soseki Natsume; translated by Aiko Ito and Graeme Wilson*

In Ghostly Japan *by Lafcadio Hearn*

Japan: An Attempt at Interpretation *by Lafcadio Hearn*

Japanese Folk-Plays: The Ink-Smeared Lady and Other Kyogen *translated by Shio Sakanishi*

Japanese Tales of Mystery & Imagination *by Edogawa Rampo; translated by James B. Harris*

Japanese Things: Being Notes on Various Subjects Connected with Japan *by Basil Hall Chamberlain*

Kappa *by Ryunosuke Akutagawa; translated by Geoffrey Bownas*

Kokoro: Hints and Echoes of Japanese Inner Life *by Lafcadio Hearn*

Kotto: Being Japanese Curios, with Sundry Cobwebs *by Lafcadio Hearn*

Kwaidan: Stories and Studies of Strange Things *by Lafacdio Hearn*

Land of the Reed Plains: Ancient Japanese Lyrics from the Manyoshu *translation and commentary by Kenneth Yasuda*

The Life of Buddha *by A. Ferdinand Herold*

CHARLES E. TUTTLE COMPANY: PUBLISHERS

Rutland, Vermont 05701 U.S.A.

Suido 1-chome, 2-6, Bunkyo-ku, Tokyo, Japan